I like the fact that the questions aren't sappy.
They're intimate but fun at the same time. These
journals feel comfortable. Good job.
                                                    T. Bruns, MN

I just moved here and the people I love most are
in Chicago. I'm sending one to my MOM, one to
my DAD, one to my GIRL and one to my MAN.
I can't wait to get them back.
                                                    S. Montiel, NJ

Very cool.
I'm anxious to read what my mom has to say
about HER teenage years.
                                                    M. Lopez, FL

Now THIS is a unique gift idea.
You really can't give or get anything
that's more personal. I would love to get one
of these from all the people I care about.
                                                    V. Dailey, AZ

I'm giving one to my dad to fill out for
my sister. Then I'll give it to my sister for
her birthday. She'll love it.
                                                    D. Brown, IL

Thank You to my family, friends, and loved ones
for your support in so many ways during the creation
of this book. I truly appreciate you all.

Let's share. This journal is dedicated to those who
seek to exchange the simplest, yet most meaningful
of gifts...the ones we carry within.

Library of Congress Cataloging-In-Publication Data available.
ISBN: 0-9720230-4-6

Sand Dune Publishing Company
P.O. Box 2995, Miller Beach, Indiana 46403
Phone: 219 938-7118   Fax 312 896-7458
email: editor@sanddunebooks.com
www.sanddunebooks.com

Words are powerful...and precious...especially when they're written by people you love. The **Between Me And You™** journal series offers a straightforward and meaningful way to get a little closer to those people.

Give it to someone you know or would like to get to know better. Inside are questions that are simple and provocative, fun to ask and fun to answer. The book is then returned to you with honest and most times, revealing responses.

Tell the recipient to have fun with it and to express themselves however they wish...with words, pictures, clippings, anything. There are also extra blank pages in the back so if you'd like to add your own VERY special questions, go for it.

On the other hand, you can tear out the pages on which there's stuff you have no need for (like this page). It's your book. And I can pretty much guarantee that this will be one you'll want to read over and over again.

And hold onto my contact information. If you get a minute, please write, call or email me and share your experience with it. Thanks.

Winston

between me and you™

GRANDMA

This book belongs to _____

and was given to my grandmother, _____

She put up with my questions and

returned it to me on _____

Sent to

Blue Tooth Speaker Water Bottle
Sent $150 with Card
Birth Cake in Mug

between me and you™

GRANDMA

Hi Grandma.

I'm giving this book to you so that you'll return it to
me. You're so very special and this is my chance to
learn a little more about who you WERE once upon
a time and who you ARE right now.

It's funny how all who touch us affect our lives in
unique ways. Especially grandparents.

Please take some time and reflect on the questions
inside and write as much or as little as you want.

I look forward to getting this back soon. And please
know that I will cherish it, not because of what you
write, but simply because you wrote.

Thanks.

Contents

When You Were A Kid

What do you remember most

about being a kid?

the times

*What were some of your favorite
things to do as a child?*

What are your favorite memories

of your father?

conversations

experiences

when you were a kid

What are some of your favorite memories of

your mother ?

characteristics

What was your *sister*(s) like
when you were growing up?

What was your brother(s) like
when you were growing up?

stories

similarities

decisions

when you were a kid

Did you ever get upset *with your parents?*
Why?

Do you remember your
childhood friends?
What are your memories?

school

neighborhood

when you were a kid

teachers

when you were a kid

What kind of student were you as a kid?
What were your favorite subjects?

report cards

why

when you were a kid

When you were a kid,
        what did you want to be when you
grew up?

Your Youth

peer pressure

responsibility

your youth

What are your memories of being

a teenager?

times

So...what were your teenage
dating experiences? Do you
remember your first date?

crushes

first kiss

your youth

Did you have any role models
when you were a teen? Who were they
and why did you look up to them?

heroes

stars

heroines

your youth

songs

your youth

What kind of music did you like as a teen?
Any favorite artists or groups?

dances

*Did you have a dream or burning desire
to have any particular experience or
adventure as a young adult?*

travels

fantasies

your youth

My Grandfather

*Tell me about the first time
you met my grandfather.*

Do you remember the first time the
two of you had your first date?
Tell me about it.

where

How *long* did you and my granddad date?

Any memorable experiences?

places

my grandfather

What are your memories of the day
you and grandfather were married?

wedding

ring

my grandfather

thrills

my grandfather

Which have been the most interesting
times during your life with my granddad?

spills

You, Then

feelings

you, then

*What do you remember most
about the time you
were pregnant with my parent?*

preparations

What are your memories of

the day my parent was born?

people

places

weather

you, then

toys

Do you have any favorite memories
of my parent as a child?

you, then

What might I be surprised to learn about
my parent when much younger?

skills

How do you think I'm similar?

or different?

attitudes

you, then

you

people

you, then

*What stands out most in your mind about the times
when you were a young woman?*

the world

For you, what was the most rewarding aspect of your life as a young woman?

What was the most
challenging?

you, then

Please tell me about the work you've done throughout your life.

fun

voluntary

profit

you, then

So far, what event in history has been the most challenging for you to live through?

national

world

personal

you, then

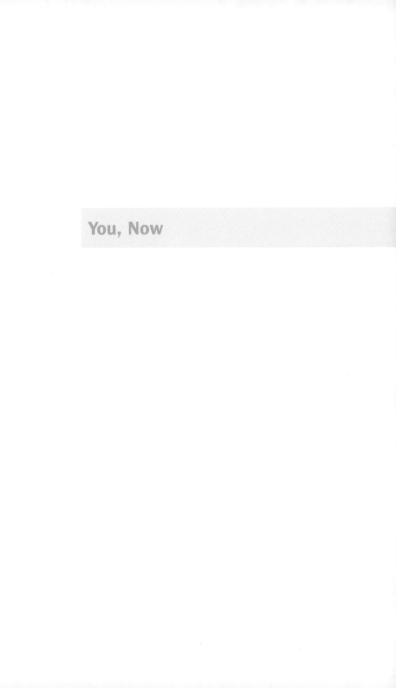

You, Now

events

people

you, now

What really, really, really makes you

happy?

situations

What are some of the things
you would still like to
accomplish?

relationships

challenges

Do you have any future plans
that you would care to share with me?

dreams

goals

you, now

Is there anything you miss about the way you lived life years ago?

In what ways has life
surprised you the most?

What do you think is your best quality?

What do you think is your

not-so-best quality?

As you think about your life so far, what
are you most proud of ?

talents

occasions

Do you have *any* regrets
that you'd care to share with me?

near

you, now

What have been your favorite travels?
Any interesting stories?

far

unusual

Is there anything you think I should know about anything? Anything at all?
Anything?

anything

you, now

If you felt the need to offer some advice to me, what would it be?

What more would you like to see me
do or learn in this lifetime?

wisdom

you, now

Other Stuff

other stuff

other stuff

other stuff

other stuff

other stuff

other stuff

other stuff

I know I've asked a lot of questions. Thanks for taking the time... and for sharing.